Online Riches in 2024

The Comprehensive Guide to Monetizing Websites, Blogging, Video, and More for Income

M.H. Marks

Table of Contents

Introduction

Welcome to "Online Riches in 2024: The Comprehensive Guide to Monetizing Websites, Blogging, Video, and More for Income." As you embark on this journey, envision a life of financial freedom, where the internet becomes your gateway to prosperity and fulfillment. Picture a future where your online endeavors not only sustain your lifestyle but elevate it to new heights, providing the autonomy to live life on your terms.

In the ever-evolving landscape of the internet, opportunities abound, waiting to be seized by those who dare to dream and act. As we stand on the threshold of 2024, the digital realm is a canvas of potential, offering fresh and exciting ways to transform your passion and expertise into a thriving source of income. The pace of technological advancement continues to accelerate, presenting novel avenues for monetization that were unthinkable just a few years ago.

Allow me to guide you through this transformative journey. My name is M.H Marks, and I've navigated the intricacies of online income generation, building successful ventures from the ground up. Through years of experience, I've honed the strategies and insights necessary to flourish in the dynamic online landscape.

In "Online Riches in 2024," I share with you a blueprint for success, providing step-by-step guidance that spans the spectrum from cultivating the right mindset to mastering the technical intricacies and leveraging automation for efficiency. This isn't just a guide; it's a personalized roadmap designed to propel you towards online success in the present year.

As you flip through these pages, consider the urgency of aligning your aspirations with the current year. The time for fresh starts and new goals is now. Your lifestyle and dreams deserve to be in sync with the opportunities the digital age offers. This book isn't just about making money online; it's about crafting a future that resonates with your vision, passions, and aspirations.

I invite you to take the first step toward your online success. Dive into the first chapter and let the journey begin. Your dreams await, and the time for forward momentum is now.

Chapter 1

Building a Strong Online Presence

Establishing Your Brand Identity

Hey there, digital trailblazer! Welcome to the first chapter of our journey toward online riches in 2024. Today, we're diving into the exciting world of building a robust online presence – the very foundation of your success in the vast realm of the internet.

Establishing Your Brand Identity
Imagine your brand as the digital fingerprint that sets you apart in the online crowd. It's not just a logo or a name; it's the personality and values that resonate with your audience. Let's break down the essentials in simple, actionable steps:

Step 1: Unveil Your Unique Self
Your brand starts with you. What makes you special? Your quirks, passions, and expertise are

the secret sauce. Take a moment to jot down what defines you.

Step 2: Define Your Message
What story do you want to tell the world? Your message should align with your values and resonate with your audience. It's the narrative that turns one-time visitors into loyal followers.

Example: If you're a fitness enthusiast, your message might be about making health accessible to everyone, regardless of their fitness level.

Step 3: Visual Identity Matters
Choose colors, fonts, and visuals that reflect your brand personality. This isn't just about looking pretty; it's about creating a visual language that your audience will instantly recognize.

Example: Think of the Nike swoosh or the golden arches of McDonald's, simple yet instantly recognizable.

Step 4: Consistency is Key
Whether you're posting on social media, writing a blog, or creating videos, maintain a consistent tone and style. This builds trust and helps your audience connect with you on a deeper level.

Example: If your brand is playful and humorous, infuse that personality into all your content.

Step 5: Be Where Your Audience Is

Identify the platforms your audience frequents. If you're targeting a younger demographic, TikTok might be your playground. For a professional audience, LinkedIn could be the sweet spot.

Example: A cooking enthusiast might find success on Instagram or YouTube, where visual content reigns supreme.

Recap: Your Brand, Your Digital Identity

So, what have we learned? Your brand is more than just a logo, it's the essence of who you are in the digital world. Unveil your unique self, craft a compelling message, choose a visual identity, be consistent, and meet your audience where they are.

Now, let's chat!
- What aspects of your personality or expertise can become part of your brand?
- Have you identified platforms where your target audience hangs out?

Crafting Compelling Content

Hey Content Creators! Now that we've laid the groundwork with a snazzy brand identity, it's time to talk about the heartbeat of your online presence, compelling content. Think of it as the magnetic force that keeps your audience hooked, scrolling, and eagerly awaiting your next masterpiece. Let's break it down into bite-sized, action-packed nuggets:

1. Know Your Audience Like Your BFF
Before you dive into content creation, get to know your audience inside out. What makes them tick? What are their pain points, dreams, and desires? Your content should be the answer to their unspoken questions.

Pro Tip: Create audience personas. Think of them as your imaginary friends – you know them so well that creating content becomes a breeze.

2. The Power of Storytelling
Humans are wired to love stories. Weave narratives into your content, personal anecdotes, client success stories, or even fictional tales that align with your brand.

Storytelling creates an emotional connection that plain facts can't match.

Example: If you're in the fitness niche, share your journey, struggles, and triumphs. Your audience will relate and root for you.

3. Visuals Speak Louder Than Words

A picture is worth a thousand words, and a snappy infographic or engaging video is worth even more online. Invest time in creating visually appealing content that stands out in the sea of information.

Pro Tip: Use tools like Canva or Adobe Spark for easy-to-create graphics and videos, even if you're not a design wizard.

4. Educate, Entertain, Engage – The Triple E Combo

Your content should serve a purpose: educate, entertain, and engage. Whether you're writing a blog post, creating a video, or posting on social media, make sure your audience gains value.

Example: If you're a tech guru, your content might teach new skills, entertain with tech humor, and engage through interactive discussions.

5. Consistency, Consistency, Consistency

Consistency isn't just for your brand – it's crucial for your content too. Whether you're posting daily, weekly, or bi-weekly, set a schedule and stick to it. Consistency builds anticipation and keeps your audience coming back.

Pro Tip: Create a content calendar. It's your roadmap to consistency.

Recap: Crafting Compelling Content Magic

So, what's the takeaway?

- Know your audience intimately.
- Embrace the power of storytelling.
- Use visuals to captivate attention.
- Educate, entertain, and engage, the Triple E Combo.
- Be consistent with your audience's favorite TV show.

Now, let's chat!

- What stories can you share that align with your brand?
- How can you make your content visually appealing?

Navigating Social Media for Maximum Exposure

Hey Social Butterflies! Ready to sprinkle some digital stardust on your online presence? In this chapter, we're delving into the vibrant universe of social media, the powerhouse for maximum exposure and connection. Let's unlock the secrets to skyrocketing your visibility in the social stratosphere:

1. Choose Your Platforms Wisely
Not all social media platforms are created equal, and neither is your target audience on every platform. Tailor your strategy by selecting the platforms where your audience hangs out. Facebook, Instagram, Twitter, LinkedIn – each has its flavor.

Example: If you're in the visual arts, Instagram and Pinterest might be your go-to platforms.

2. Optimize Your Profiles for Pizzazz
Your social media profiles are your digital business cards. Sprinkle them with a dash of personality, a captivating bio, a snazzy profile picture, and a link to your website. Make it easy for your audience to know who you are and what you're about.

Pro Tip: Use keywords relevant to your niche for discoverability.

3. Content is King, Engagement is Queen
Create content that not only stops the scroll but also sparks conversations. Engage with your audience through comments, likes, and shares. Social media is a two-way street, and the more you engage, the more your audience will too.

Example: Ask questions, run polls, and share user-generated content to foster a sense of community.

4. Hashtags: Your Social GPS
Harness the power of hashtags to amplify your reach. Research and use relevant hashtags to make your content discoverable to a broader audience. But remember, it's quality over quantity, choose hashtags wisely.

Pro Tip: Create a branded hashtag for your community.

5. Consistent Posting: The Algorithm's Best Friend
Social media algorithms love consistency. Develop a posting schedule that aligns with your audience's online habits. Whether it's daily,

bi-weekly, or a couple of times a week, stick to it like clockwork.

Example: Use scheduling tools like Buffer or Hootsuite to maintain consistency without the daily hustle.

Recap: Social Media Mastery Unleashed

In a nutshell:
- Choose platforms wisely based on your audience.
- Optimize your profiles for that wow factor.
- Create engaging content that sparks conversations.
- Use hashtags strategically for discoverability.
- Embrace the magic of consistent posting.

Now, let's chat!
- What's your favorite social media platform, and why?
- How can you infuse more personality into your social media profiles?

Unlock the secrets to skyrocketing your visibility in the social stratosphere

Chapter 2

Creating and Monetizing a Website

Website Development Essentials

Hello Web Wizards! In this chapter, we're stepping into the digital realm where your dreams take shape, website creation and the art of turning it into a money-making machine. Buckle up; we're about to demystify the essentials of website development:

1. Choose the Right Domain Name
Your domain name is your digital address, make it memorable. Keep it short, easy to spell, and reflective of your brand. Use domain extensions like .com, .net, or .org for a professional touch.

Pro Tip: Check domain availability early; you don't want to fall in love with a name that's already taken.

2. Select a Reliable Web Hosting Provider

Think of your hosting provider as the landlord of your digital storefront. Choose one with reliable uptime, excellent customer support, and the right features for your needs.

Example: Popular hosting providers include Bluehost, SiteGround, and HostGator.

3. Set Up a User-Friendly Design

Your website should be a welcoming space for visitors. Opt for a clean, intuitive design with easy navigation. Mobile responsiveness is non-negotiable, many users access websites on their phones.

Pro Tip: Platforms like WordPress, Wix, or Squarespace offer user-friendly templates for a quick start.

4. Craft Compelling Content: It's Not Just for Blogs

Whether you're selling products, services, or ideas, your website's content is the gateway to audience engagement. Use attention-grabbing headlines, captivating images, and concise, persuasive copy.

Example: If you're a photographer, showcase a portfolio that tells your visual story.

5. Integrate Monetization Strategies

Let's talk business! Monetize your website through various channels, ads, affiliate marketing, or selling products/services directly. Strategically place ads or create a dedicated "Shop" section to guide your audience toward conversion.

Pro Tip: Balance monetization with user experience, too many ads can turn visitors away.

6. Implement SEO Best Practices

Search Engine Optimization (SEO) is your ticket to being discovered on the vast internet. Use relevant keywords, create meta descriptions, and optimize images to improve your website's visibility on search engines.

Example: If you're a fitness coach, optimize for keywords like "home workouts" or "healthy recipes."

Recap: Your Website, Your Digital Empire

To sum it up:
- Choose a memorable domain name.
- Select a reliable hosting provider.
- Design a user-friendly website.
- Craft compelling content that resonates.
- Integrate smart monetization strategies.

- Implement SEO for discoverability.

Now, let's chat!
- What's your dream domain name?
- Have you thought about the design elements that reflect your brand?

In our next chapter, we're delving into the world of effective content strategies. Get ready to transform your website into a captivating destination! Your digital empire is one step closer to reality.

Effective Content Strategies

Greetings Content Architects! Now that your digital space is set up, it's time to fill it with content that captivates, resonates, and converts. Let's dive into the art and science of effective content strategies:

1. Know Your Audience's Hunger

Before you hit the keyboard, understand what your audience craves. What questions are they asking? What problems are they trying to solve? Your content should be the answer they're seeking.

Pro Tip: Engage with your audience through surveys, comments, and social media to uncover their burning questions.

2. Create a Content Calendar

Consistency is your secret weapon. Develop a content calendar that maps out what you'll publish and when. This not only keeps you organized but also ensures a steady flow of valuable content for your audience.

Example: If you're a lifestyle blogger, plan seasonal content, such as holiday guides or summer wellness tips.

3. Mix Up Your Content Types

Variety is the spice of content. Mix up your content types, blog posts, videos, infographics, podcasts, to cater to different preferences. Some people love to read, while others prefer to listen or watch.

Pro Tip: Repurpose content across different mediums. Turn a blog post into a podcast episode or create video snippets for social media.

4. Engage and Interact with Your Audience

Your content isn't a monologue; it's a conversation. Respond to comments, ask questions, and encourage your audience to share their thoughts. The more engaged your audience is, the stronger your community becomes.

Example: If you're a tech guru, ask your audience about their favorite gadgets or common tech problems they'd like help with.

5. SEO Isn't Just a Buzzword

Search Engine Optimization (SEO) isn't just for the tech-savvy. Use keywords naturally in your content, create compelling meta descriptions, and structure your content for readability. SEO helps your content shine in the vast online landscape.

Pro Tip: Use tools like Google Keyword Planner or SEMrush to identify high-ranking keywords in your niche.

6. Tell Stories That Stick
Stories have a magical way of embedding themselves in memory. Whether you're sharing personal anecdotes, case studies, or client success stories, storytelling adds a human touch to your content.

Example: If you're a travel blogger, narrate your adventures with vivid details and personal reflections.

Recap: Crafting Content That Converts

Quick recap:
- Know your audience's needs intimately.
- Develop a content calendar for consistency.
- Diversify your content types for wider appeal.
- Engage and interact with your audience.
- Optimize content for SEO visibility.
- Tell stories that leave a lasting impression.

Now, let's chat!
- What types of content resonate most with your audience?

- How can you incorporate storytelling into your content strategy?

In our next installment, we're unwrapping the secrets of monetization through ads, affiliate marketing, and more. Get ready to turn your captivating content into a revenue stream! Your journey to online riches is gaining momentum.

Implementing Revenue Streams: Ads, Affiliate Marketing, and More

Greetings, Money-Makers! Now that your website is adorned with compelling content, let's talk about turning those efforts into cold, hard cash. In this chapter, we're unpacking the world of revenue streams, from ads to affiliate marketing and beyond:

1. Monetize with Strategic Ads

Ads can be your website's best friend if used wisely. Strategically place display ads or sponsored content without overwhelming your audience. Balance is key – too many ads can deter visitors.

Pro Tip: Consider platforms like Google AdSense or Media.net for seamless ad integration.

2. Dive into Affiliate Marketing

Affiliate marketing is like having a sales team working for you around the clock. Promote products or services related to your niche and earn a commission for every sale made through your unique affiliate link.

Example: If you're a fitness blogger, partner with fitness equipment brands and share your affiliate link with your audience.

3. Create and Sell Digital Products
Turn your expertise into digital gold. Create e-books, online courses, or downloadable resources that provide value to your audience. Digital products have the potential for high profit margins.

Pro Tip: Platforms like Gumroad or Teachable make it easy to sell digital products directly from your website.

4. Offer Memberships or Subscriptions
Build a loyal community by offering premium content through memberships or subscriptions. Provide exclusive access to valuable content, live sessions, or special perks for your paying members.

Example: If you're a finance expert, offer premium financial planning resources to your subscribers.

5. Sponsored Content and Partnerships
Collaborate with brands relevant to your niche for sponsored content. This could include

product reviews, sponsored posts, or even partnerships for exclusive content.

Pro Tip: Choose partnerships that align with your brand to maintain authenticity.

6. Donations and Crowdfunding

If your content adds significant value to your audience, some may be willing to support you directly. Set up donation options or explore crowdfunding platforms to gather financial support.

Example: If you run a niche blog or provide free resources, your audience might appreciate the option to contribute.

Recap: Turning Clicks into Cash

To sum it up:
- Strategically incorporate ads without overwhelming your audience.
- Leverage affiliate marketing to earn commissions.
- Create and sell digital products for high-profit potential.
- Offer memberships or subscriptions for exclusive content.
- Collaborate with brands for sponsored content and partnerships.

- Explore donations or crowdfunding for direct support.

Now, let's chat!
- Which revenue streams align best with your website's theme?
- Have you considered collaborating with brands for sponsored content?

Chapter 3

Mastering the Art of Blogging

Starting and Growing a Successful Blog

Greetings Blogging Aficionados! It's time to roll up our sleeves and dive into the heart of online expression, blogging. In this chapter, we're unlocking the secrets of not just starting a blog but nurturing it into a flourishing digital space. Let's embark on this exciting journey:

1. Find Your Blogging Niche

Your blog is your digital canvas, and your niche is the palette. Identify a topic you're passionate about and that resonates with your audience. It's not just about finding a niche; it's about finding your unique angle within it.

Pro Tip: Aim for a niche that aligns with your expertise and has an audience hungry for content.

2. Choose the Right Blogging Platform

Selecting the right platform is like picking the perfect paintbrush. WordPress, Blogger, Medium, each has its strengths. WordPress, for example, offers flexibility and customization options.

Example: If you're focusing on written content, Medium might be an excellent starting point.

3. Craft an Engaging About Page

Your About page is the story behind the artist. Share your journey, passions, and what readers can expect from your blog. Make it relatable and human, your audience wants to connect with the person behind the words.

Pro Tip: Include a professional photo to put a face to the name.

4. Develop a Consistent Posting Schedule

Consistency is the rhythm of a successful blog. Whether it's once a week or thrice a month, set a posting schedule and stick to it. Regular updates keep your audience engaged and coming back for more.

Example: If you're a food blogger, you might post new recipes every Wednesday.

5. Optimize Your Content for SEO

SEO isn't just for the tech-savvy; it's the brushstroke that brings your blog to life on search engines. Use relevant keywords, create meta descriptions, and focus on writing content that genuinely serves your audience.

Pro Tip: Regularly update and republish older blog posts to keep content fresh.

6. Build a Community through Engagement

Blogging is a conversation. Respond to comments, ask questions, and encourage your readers to share their thoughts. A thriving community not only boosts your blog's visibility but also makes the journey more enjoyable.

Example: If you're a travel blogger, ask your audience about their favorite travel destinations.

Recap: Crafting a Blogging Masterpiece

To summarize:
- Identify a niche aligned with your passion and audience interest.
- Choose the right blogging platform for your needs.
- Craft a compelling About page to connect with your audience.
- Develop a consistent posting schedule.

- Optimize your content for SEO visibility.
- Build a vibrant community through engagement.

Now, let's chat!
- What's your blog's niche, and why did you choose it?
- How can you enhance engagement within your blogging community?

In our next chapter, we're delving into the strategies for monetizing your blog effectively. Get ready to turn your creative passion into a sustainable income stream! Your journey to mastering the art of blogging is reaching new heights.

Monetization Strategies for Bloggers

Hello Blogging Maestros! Now that your blog is alive with captivating content and a buzzing community, let's talk about the thrilling part – turning your passion into profit. In this chapter, we're exploring diverse and effective monetization strategies for bloggers:

1. Strategic Ad Placement

Ads are the classic monetization route. Strategically place display ads or sponsored content within your blog. Be mindful not to clutter your space, as a seamless user experience is key.

Pro Tip: Balance ad density to avoid overwhelming your readers.

2. Affiliate Marketing Magic

Turn your recommendations into revenue through affiliate marketing. Promote products or services related to your niche and earn a commission for every sale made through your unique affiliate link.

Example: If you're a beauty blogger, review your favorite skincare products and include affiliate links.

3. Create and Sell Your Products

Leverage your expertise by creating and selling your digital or physical products. E-books, online courses, merchandise, the possibilities are vast, and the profit margins can be substantial.

Pro Tip: Tailor your products to address specific pain points within your niche.

4. Offer Premium Memberships

Build an exclusive club by offering premium memberships. Provide your members with extra perks, bonus content, Q&A sessions, or early access. This strategy fosters a sense of belonging and generates recurring revenue.

Example: If you're a finance blogger, offer premium financial advice to your members.

5. Sponsored Content Collaborations

Collaborate with brands for sponsored content. Write posts, and reviews, or create content that features a brand's product or service. Ensure that the partnership aligns with your blog's niche and maintains authenticity.

Pro Tip: disclose sponsored content to maintain transparency with your audience.

6. Freelance Writing Opportunities

Your blog is a showcase of your writing skills. Leverage it to attract freelance writing opportunities. Guest posting or contributing to other platforms can bring in additional income.

Example: If you're a travel blogger, pitch your expertise to travel magazines or websites.

7. Online Courses and Workshops

Share your knowledge through online courses or workshops. Whether it's a step-by-step guide to mastering photography or a writing workshop, turn your expertise into valuable educational content.

Pro Tip: Platforms like Teachable or Udemy provide user-friendly options for hosting online courses.

Recap: Monetizing Your Blogging Craft

To sum it up:
- Strategically incorporate ads without compromising user experience.
- Harness the power of affiliate marketing for commission-based earnings.
- Create and sell digital or physical products related to your niche.

- Offer premium memberships with exclusive perks.
- Collaborate with brands for sponsored content.
- Explore freelance writing opportunities.
- Host online courses or workshops to share your expertise.

Now, let's chat!
- Which monetization strategy resonates most with your blog?
- How can you align your chosen strategies with your blog's niche?

Building and Engaging with Your Blogging Community

Greetings Community Builders! In this chapter, we're delving into the heart and soul of your blog, your community. Building and nurturing an engaged audience is not just about numbers; it's about creating a loyal tribe that amplifies your blog's impact. Let's embark on the journey of community building:

1. Foster Open Communication
Communication is the bridge that connects you with your audience. Encourage comments, respond to questions, and create a space where your readers feel heard. This open dialogue not only builds trust but also makes your blog feel like a living, breathing community.

Pro Tip: Ask open-ended questions at the end of your posts to spark conversations.

2. Create a Welcoming Environment
Your blog is your digital home. Make it warm and inviting. Ensure that your design is user-friendly, your content is easily accessible, and your navigation is intuitive. A welcoming environment encourages visitors to explore and return.

Example: If you're a travel blogger, organize your content by destinations for easy navigation.

3. Encourage User-Generated Content
Empower your community to contribute. Whether it's through guest posts, shared stories, or even user-generated challenges, involving your audience in the creation process deepens their connection with your blog.

Pro Tip: Feature user-generated content regularly to showcase the diversity within your community.

4. Host Virtual Events and Q&A Sessions
Bring your community together through virtual events or Q&A sessions. It could be a live webinar, a Twitter chat, or an Instagram Live session. These real-time interactions create a sense of immediacy and intimacy.

Example: If you're a parenting blogger, host a live Q&A session on Facebook about common parenting challenges.

5. Implement Loyalty Programs
Reward your most engaged readers with loyalty programs. Offer exclusive perks, early access to content, or special discounts on your products

or services. Recognizing and appreciating your community fosters a sense of belonging.

Pro Tip: Create a dedicated space on your blog to highlight and celebrate your most engaged readers.

6. Showcase Behind-the-Scenes
Peel back the curtain and let your audience see the human side of your blog. Share behind-the-scenes glimpses, your creative process, or personal stories. This transparency builds a genuine connection with your community.

Example: If you're a lifestyle blogger, share a "day in the life" post or a behind-the-scenes video.

Recap: Nurturing Your Blogging Family

To recap:
- Foster open communication to build trust.
- Create a welcoming environment for your readers.
- Encourage user-generated content for diversity.
- Host virtual events and Q&A sessions for real-time interactions.

- Implement loyalty programs to recognize and reward engagement.
- Showcase behind the scenes to build a genuine connection.

Now, let's chat!
- How do you currently engage with your blog community?
- What initiatives can you implement to foster a stronger sense of community?

In our next chapter, we're exploring the world of e-commerce and how you can seamlessly integrate it into your blogging universe. Get ready to unlock new possibilities! Your journey to mastering the art of blogging is becoming a vibrant tapestry of creativity and connection.

Building and nurturing an engaged audience is not just about numbers; it's about creating a loyal tribe that amplifies your blog's impact.

Chapter 4

Leveraging Video Content for Income

Creating Engaging Videos

Hello Video Visionaries! In this chapter, we're diving into the dynamic world of video content, a powerhouse for engagement and income. Whether you're a seasoned creator or just stepping into the realm of moving images, we'll explore how to create engaging videos that not only captivate your audience but also contribute to your revenue streams:

1. Choose Your Platform Wisely
Selecting the right platform is like choosing the stage for your performance. YouTube, TikTok, Instagram, or even your own website – consider where your audience is and where your content will shine the brightest.

Example: If you're creating in-depth tutorials, YouTube might be your stage. For short, snappy content, TikTok could be the sweet spot.

2. Craft Engaging Video Topics

Your video's success begins with compelling topics. Identify what resonates with your audience and aligns with your niche. Whether it's educational, entertaining, or a mix of both, ensure your content provides value.

Pro Tip: Research trending topics within your niche to stay relevant.

3. Pay Attention to Video Quality

While you don't need Hollywood-level production, video quality matters. Invest in decent lighting, clear audio, and a stable camera setup. A polished video not only looks more professional but also keeps viewers engaged.

Example: Natural light and a smartphone can suffice for beginners. Upgrade equipment as your budget allows.

4. Create Consistent Branding

Consistent branding across your videos creates a visual identity that viewers can recognize. Use a consistent color scheme, logo placement, and video intro/outro. This builds brand recognition and trust.

Pro Tip: Use video editing tools to add a professional touch, even if you're a one-person production team.

5. Engage with Your Audience

Video content is a two-way street. Encourage viewers to comment, ask questions, and share their thoughts. Respond to comments and foster a sense of community. This engagement not only boosts your video's visibility but also strengthens your connection with the audience.

Example: End your video with a call-to-action, inviting viewers to comment on their thoughts or experiences related to the video.

6. Explore Monetization Features

Most video platforms offer various monetization features. From ad revenue to channel memberships and sponsored content, explore the options available. As your audience grows, these features can contribute significantly to your income.

Pro Tip: Research and understand the specific monetization features of the platform you're using.

Recap: Lights, Camera, Engagement!

In summary:
- Choose the right platform for your content.
- Craft engaging video topics aligned with your audience.
- Pay attention to video quality for a polished look.
- Create consistent branding for brand recognition.
- Engage with your audience through comments and discussions.
- Explore monetization features to turn your videos into income streams.

Now, let's chat!
- What type of video content resonates most with your audience?
- How can you enhance the consistency of your video branding?

In our next chapter, we're stepping into the world of e-commerce strategies for video creators. Get ready to turn your engaging videos into a revenue-generating machine! Your journey to leveraging video content for income is reaching new heights.

Platforms and Channels for Video Monetization

Greetings Video Entrepreneurs! Now that you've mastered the art of creating engaging videos, let's explore the diverse platforms and channels that can transform your visual content into a lucrative income stream. From established giants to emerging stars, here are some platforms and channels to consider:

1. YouTube: The Video Kingdom

Monetization Features:
- Ad Revenue: Enable ads on your videos and earn a share of the revenue.
- YouTube Partner Program (YPP): Unlock additional features, like channel memberships and merchandise shelf, by joining YPP.
- Super Chat: Allow viewers to purchase highlighted messages during live streams.

Pro Tip: Consistency is key on YouTube. Regular uploads and engagement with your audience contribute to success.

2. TikTok: Short-Form Magic

Monetization Features:
- TikTok Creator Fund: Earn money based on views and engagement metrics.
- Live Gifts: Receive gifts from viewers during live sessions.
- Brand Partnerships: Collaborate with brands for sponsored content.

Example: TikTok's engaging short-form content is perfect for quick tutorials, behind-the-scenes glimpses, and entertaining skits.

3. Instagram: Visual Storytelling

Monetization Features:
- IGTV Ads: Monetize longer videos with in-stream ads.
- Sponsored Content: Partner with brands for sponsored posts or Stories.
- Instagram Shop: Sell products directly through your profile.

Pro Tip: Leverage Instagram's visual appeal for lifestyle, travel, and beauty content.

4. Patreon: Community Support

Monetization Features:
- Memberships: Offer exclusive content to paying patrons.
- Tiers: Create different membership levels with varying perks.
- Direct Support: Allow patrons to contribute one-time payments or ongoing support.

Example: Patreon is ideal for creators who want to build a dedicated community and offer premium content.

5. Twitch: Live Streaming Haven

Monetization Features:
- Subscriptions: Earn money through paid subscriber tiers.
- Bits and Cheers: Viewers can purchase and send virtual items during streams.
- Ad Revenue: Twitch offers an ad revenue-sharing program.

Pro Tip: Twitch is excellent for live streaming content, especially in the gaming, music, and creative niches.

6. Facebook: Social Monetization Hub

Monetization Features:
- Ad Breaks: Earn money from short ads during videos.
- Brand Collabs Manager: Connect with brands for collaboration opportunities.
- Fan Subscriptions: Allow fans to support you with monthly payments.

Example: Facebook's diverse user base makes it suitable for a wide range of content, from tutorials to vlogs.

Recap: Monetizing Across Platforms

To recap:
- YouTube offers a variety of monetization features, including ad revenue and memberships.
- TikTok is perfect for short-form content with options like the Creator Fund and live gifts.
- Instagram provides monetization avenues through IGTV, sponsored content, and direct selling.
- Patreon focuses on building a community with membership tiers and direct support.

- Twitch excels in live streaming, offering subscriptions, virtual items, and ad revenue.
- Facebook offers ad breaks, brand collaborations, and fan subscriptions for diverse content.

Now, let's chat!
- Which platform aligns best with your content and audience?
- How can you strategically diversify your presence across these platforms?

In our next chapter, we'll explore effective e-commerce strategies for video creators. Get ready to unlock new possibilities in the world of online income! Your journey to leveraging video content for income is on the verge of exciting breakthroughs.

Monetizing Live Streaming and Video Series

Greetings Content Architects! In this chapter, we're delving into the exciting realms of live streaming and video series, exploring strategies to not only captivate your audience but also turn those captivating moments into revenue streams. Let's dive into the art of monetizing live content and serialized videos:

1. Live Streaming Monetization Strategies

a. Subscriptions:
- Platforms like Twitch and YouTube allow viewers to subscribe to your channel for exclusive perks.
- Subscriptions can offer benefits like custom emotes, badges, and access to subscriber-only content.

b. Donations and Tips:
- Enable features that allow viewers to send donations or tips during your live streams.
- Express gratitude and acknowledge donors during your streams to encourage further support.

c. Sponsored Live Streams:

- Partner with brands for sponsored live streams where you showcase their products or services.
- Ensure a seamless integration of sponsored content to maintain viewer engagement.

d. Virtual Gifts:

- Platforms like Facebook and TikTok offer virtual gifts that viewers can purchase and send during live sessions.
- Create an engaging system to acknowledge and appreciate viewers who send virtual gifts.

2. Monetizing Video Series

a. Ad Sponsorships:

- Integrate sponsored ads into your video series, either through pre-roll or mid-roll placements.
- Ensure that sponsored content aligns with the theme and interests of your audience.

b. Patreon or Memberships:

- Create a membership or subscription model for your video series on platforms like Patreon or YouTube.

- Offer exclusive perks to subscribers, such as early access, behind-the-scenes content, or member-only Q&A sessions.

c. Product Placement:
- Strategically incorporate product placements within your video series.
- Ensure that product placements feel natural and enhance the viewer's experience.

d. Premium Content Access:
- Implement a paywall system for premium content within your video series.
- Viewers can purchase or subscribe to access high-value, exclusive episodes.

3. Engage and Interact Strategically

a. Interactive Polls and Q&A:
- Integrate polls and Q&A sessions during live streams to encourage viewer participation.
- Use interactive elements strategically, especially during sponsored content to gauge audience preferences.

b. Community Challenges:
- Initiate challenges within your video series and live streams.

- Encourage viewers to participate and showcase their creations, with the potential to feature them in future content.

c. Cross-Promotions:
- Collaborate with other creators for cross-promotional opportunities.
- This can expand your reach and introduce your content to new audiences, potentially increasing monetization opportunities.

Recap: Turning Live Moments into Income

In summary:
Live Streaming:
- Utilize subscriptions, donations, and virtual gifts for live stream monetization.
- Explore sponsored live streams for brand collaborations.

Video Series:
- Incorporate ad sponsorships and product placements.
- Offer memberships, Patreon, or premium content access for dedicated viewers.

Engagement Strategies:
- Use interactive elements like polls and challenges.
- Explore cross-promotions with other creators for mutual benefit.

Now, let's chat!
- How can you incorporate interactive elements to enhance your live streams?
- Which monetization strategy aligns best with your video series concept?

In our next chapter, we're unraveling effective e-commerce strategies for video creators. Get ready to seamlessly integrate commerce into your content journey! Your path to monetizing live streaming and video series is on the brink of exciting possibilities.

Exploring strategies to not only captivate your audience but also turn those captivating moments into revenue streams.

Chapter 5

Exploring E-commerce Opportunities

Setting Up an Online Store

Greetings Digital Entrepreneurs! In this chapter, we're venturing into the expansive realm of e-commerce, discovering the myriad opportunities to transform your content into a thriving online store. From merchandising to digital products, we'll explore how to set up an online store that seamlessly aligns with your brand and content:

1. Define Your E-commerce Niche

a. Merchandise:
- Design and sell physical merchandise related to your content, think branded apparel, accessories, or custom products.
- Leverage print-on-demand services for a hassle-free inventory solution.

b. Digital Products:
- Create and sell digital products such as e-books, online courses, or downloadable resources.
- Tailor your digital products to complement your content and audience's interests.

2. Choose the Right E-commerce Platform

a. Shopify:
- Ideal for beginners, offering user-friendly interfaces and a range of customizable templates.
- Integrated tools for inventory management, payments, and analytics.

b. WooCommerce (WordPress):
- Perfect for those already using WordPress, seamlessly integrating with existing websites.
- Customizable and offers a range of plugins for added functionalities.

c. Etsy:
- Suited for creators focused on handmade or unique products.
- Leverage Etsy's established marketplace and audience for your products.

3. Design a User-Friendly Online Store

a. Clean Layout and Navigation:
- Ensure a visually appealing layout with easy navigation.
- Simplify the purchasing process with clear calls to action.

b. High-Quality Product Images:
- Showcase your products with high-quality images from multiple angles.
- Provide detailed descriptions to enhance customer understanding.

c. Secure Payment Options:
- Integrate secure payment gateways to build trust with your customers.
- Offer various payment options for customer convenience.

4. Implement Marketing and Promotions

a. Social Media Integration:
- Leverage your existing social media platforms to promote your online store.
- Use platforms like Instagram Shopping to directly tag and sell products.

b. Email Marketing Campaigns:
- Build an email subscriber list to keep customers informed about new products and promotions.
- Implement targeted email campaigns for personalized outreach.

c. Limited-Time Offers and Discounts:
- Create a sense of urgency with limited-time offers and exclusive discounts.
- Implement seasonal promotions to drive sales during peak times.

5. Provide Excellent Customer Support

a. Clear Communication:
- Communicate transparently about product details, shipping, and returns.
- Promptly respond to customer inquiries and feedback.

b. Easy Returns and Exchanges:
- Implement a hassle-free return and exchange policy.
- Prioritize customer satisfaction to build long-term loyalty.

6. Analytics and Optimization

a. Track Performance:
- Utilize analytics tools to track the performance of your online store.
- Monitor sales, customer behavior, and popular products for strategic decisions.

b. Continuous Optimization:
- Regularly update and optimize your online store based on analytics insights.
- Implement improvements to enhance the user experience and boost sales.

Recap: Crafting Your E-commerce Empire

To summarize:
- Define your e-commerce niche, whether it's merchandise or digital products.
- Choose the right e-commerce platform for your needs.
- Design a user-friendly online store with a clean layout and secure payment options.
- Implement marketing strategies through social media, email campaigns, and promotions.
- Prioritize excellent customer support and easy returns/exchanges.
- Utilize analytics to track performance and continuously optimize your online store.

Now, let's chat!
- What products or digital goods align with your content and audience?
- How can you integrate promotions and marketing to drive traffic to your online store?

In our next chapter, we'll explore advanced e-commerce strategies to elevate your online store to new heights. Get ready for a journey into the intricacies of successful digital commerce! Your venture into e-commerce opportunities is poised for exceptional growth.

Product Selection and Marketing

Greetings E-commerce Pioneers! Now that you've set up the foundation of your online store, let's delve into the art of selecting products that resonate with your audience and crafting impactful marketing strategies to propel your e-commerce venture forward:

1. Strategic Product Selection

a. Align with Your Brand:
- Choose products that seamlessly align with your brand and content.
- Maintain consistency in design, messaging, and overall aesthetic.

b. Understand Your Audience:
- Identify the preferences and needs of your target audience.
- Consider conducting surveys or polls to gather insights.

c. Diversify Your Offerings:
- Provide a variety of products to cater to different preferences.
- Diversification minimizes risk and appeals to a broader customer base.

2. *Compelling Product Descriptions*

a. Highlight Benefits:
- Clearly articulate the benefits of each product.
- Address how the product solves a problem or enhances the customer's life.

b. Use Descriptive Language:
- Paint a vivid picture with descriptive language.
- Help customers envision the experience of owning or using the product.

c. Incorporate SEO Keywords:
- Optimize product descriptions with relevant SEO keywords.
- Enhance visibility on search engines and attract organic traffic.

3. *Visual Appeal: High-Quality Images and Videos*

a. Professional Product Photography:
- Invest in professional-quality images showcasing your products.
- Multiple angles and close-ups provide a comprehensive view.

b. Video Demonstrations:
- Create video content demonstrating product features or uses.
- Videos offer a dynamic way to engage and inform potential customers.

c. User-Generated Content:
- Encourage customers to share photos or videos of them using your products.
- User-generated content builds authenticity and trust.

4. *Leverage Social Media for Marketing*

a. Visual Storytelling:
- Craft visually appealing social media posts that tell a story.
- Share the journey of your products, from creation to satisfied customers.

b. Influencer Collaborations:
- Partner with influencers relevant to your niche.
- Influencers can amplify your products to their engaged audience.

c. Social Media Advertising:
- Utilize targeted social media ads to reach specific demographics.

- Experiment with different ad formats and analyze performance.

5. *Email Marketing Campaigns*

a. Build an Engaged Subscriber List:
- Grow an email subscriber list through your online store and social media.
- Offer incentives like exclusive discounts for subscriptions.

b. Personalized Campaigns:
- Implement personalized email campaigns based on customer preferences.
- Segment your audience for targeted promotions.

c. Limited-Time Offers:
- Create a sense of urgency with limited-time offers in email campaigns.
- Encourage subscribers to take immediate action.

6. *Customer Reviews and Testimonials*

a. Encourage Reviews:
- Promptly ask customers for reviews after their purchase.
- Positive reviews build trust and influence potential buyers.

b. *Showcase Testimonials:*
- Highlight customer testimonials on your website and marketing materials.
- Real-life experiences add credibility to your products.

7. Analytics for Informed Decision-Making

a. Track Sales Performance:
- Utilize analytics tools to monitor product sales and performance.
- Identify top-performing products and optimize accordingly.

b. Customer Behavior Analysis:
- Analyze customer behavior on your website.
- Understand what products attract the most attention and adjust your strategy.

Recap: Elevating Your Product Selection and Marketing Game

In summary:
Strategic Product Selection:
- Align products with your brand and audience preferences.
- Diversify offerings to appeal to a broader customer base.

Compelling Product Descriptions:
- Highlight benefits and use descriptive language.
- Optimize descriptions with SEO keywords.

Visual Appeal:
- Invest in professional product photography.
- Use video content and encourage user-generated content.

Social Media Marketing:
- Craft visually appealing posts and collaborate with influencers.
- Utilize targeted social media advertising.

Email Marketing:
- Build an engaged subscriber list.
- Implement personalized campaigns and limited-time offers.

Customer Reviews and Testimonials:
- Encourage and showcase customer reviews.
- Leverage testimonials for added credibility.

Analytics:
- Track sales performance and customer behavior.
- Make informed decisions based on analytics insights.

Now, let's chat!
- How can you enhance the visual appeal of your product listings?
- Which marketing strategy aligns best with your brand and audience?

In our next chapter, we'll explore advanced e-commerce strategies to propel your online store into sustained success. Get ready for a deep dive into the intricacies of thriving in the digital marketplace! Your journey into product selection and marketing is set to reach new heights.

Maximizing Sales and Profits

Hello Sales Maestros! In this chapter, we're diving into the strategies and tactics that will elevate your sales game and boost your profits. Whether you're selling products, services, or a combination of both, let's explore ways to maximize your sales and reap the financial rewards:

1. Know Your Target Audience Inside Out

Understanding your audience is the cornerstone of successful sales. Dive deep into their demographics, preferences, and pain points. Tailor your offerings to precisely meet their needs, making your products or services irresistible.

Example: If you're selling fitness gear, know the specific preferences and fitness goals of your audience.

2. Optimize Your Pricing Strategy

Pricing is a delicate dance between value and affordability. Ensure your pricing reflects the perceived value of your offerings. Consider bundling products, offering discounts, or creating tiered pricing structures to cater to different segments of your audience.

Pro Tip: Test different pricing strategies to find the sweet spot that maximizes sales without compromising profit margins.

3. Implement Cross-Selling and Upselling

Encourage customers to explore more of what you offer. Cross-selling suggests related products, while upselling encourages customers to choose a higher-tier option. These strategies not only increase the average transaction value but also enhance the overall shopping experience.

Example: If you're selling cameras, cross-sell by suggesting complementary accessories, and upsell by showcasing a premium model.

4. Leverage Limited-Time Offers and Scarcity

Create a sense of urgency with limited-time offers and scarcity. Whether it's a flash sale, exclusive discounts for early birds, or limited stock, these tactics prompt customers to make purchasing decisions swiftly.

Pro Tip: Clearly communicate the urgency and scarcity to drive immediate action.

5. Build Trust Through Reviews and Testimonials

Trust is the currency of online sales. Showcase customer reviews and testimonials prominently. Positive feedback builds confidence in your products or services, making potential customers more likely to convert.

Example: Feature customer testimonials on product pages, and encourage customers to leave reviews after their purchase.

6. Invest in a Seamless Checkout Process

A complicated checkout process can be a conversion killer. Streamline the buying journey, making it as easy and frictionless as possible. Eliminate unnecessary steps, and offer multiple payment options for convenience.

Pro Tip: Implement a guest checkout option to reduce barriers for first-time customers.

7. Implement Data-Driven Marketing

Leverage data analytics to refine your marketing strategies. Analyze customer behavior, track sales trends, and use this data to optimize your marketing efforts. A data-driven approach ensures you're making informed decisions to maximize sales.

Example: Use analytics tools to identify high-performing marketing channels and allocate your budget accordingly.

Recap: Sales Mastery Unleashed

To summarize:
- Understand your target audience deeply.
- Optimize your pricing strategy for value and affordability.
- Implement cross-selling and upselling tactics.
- Create urgency with limited-time offers and scarcity.
- Build trust through customer reviews and testimonials.
- Streamline the checkout process for a seamless experience.
- Harness the power of data-driven marketing for continuous improvement.

Now, let's chat!
- What pricing strategies align best with your products or services?
- How can you enhance the trust-building elements on your sales platform?

In our next chapter, we're delving into advanced e-commerce strategies to take your sales and profits to new heights. Get ready for the next level of financial success! Your journey to maximizing sales and profits is gaining momentum.

Chapter 6

Podcasting for Profit

Launching a Successful Podcast

Greetings Podcast Pioneers! In this chapter, we're embarking on the exciting journey of launching a podcast that not only captivates audiences but also becomes a lucrative avenue for profit. Whether you're a seasoned podcaster or a beginner with a mic, let's explore the key steps to launching a successful podcast and turning it into a profitable venture:

1. Define Your Podcast Niche and Audience
Before hitting the record button, clarify your podcast's niche and target audience. What unique angle or expertise will your podcast bring to the table? Tailor your content to resonate with a specific audience, making your podcast a go-to resource for a particular niche.

Example: If you're passionate about personal finance, your niche could be budgeting tips for young professionals.

2. Craft Compelling and Consistent Content

Consistency is key in the podcasting realm. Develop a content plan that aligns with your niche and audience interests. Craft compelling episode topics that provide value, entertain, or educate your listeners. A well-thought-out content strategy keeps your audience engaged and coming back for more.

Pro Tip: Plan and create an editorial calendar to maintain consistency.

3. Invest in Quality Audio Equipment

Clear and crisp audio is non-negotiable in the podcasting world. Invest in quality microphones, headphones, and recording/editing software. A professional-sounding podcast not only attracts listeners but also enhances your credibility.

Example: Entry-level USB microphones like the Blue Yeti are a great starting point for podcasters on a budget.

4. Design an Eye-Catching Podcast Cover

Your podcast cover is the first impression on potential listeners. Design a visually appealing and professional cover that reflects the tone and content of your podcast. A well-designed cover can significantly impact your podcast's discoverability.

Pro Tip: Use contrasting colors and legible fonts to ensure visibility, especially on smaller screens.

5. *Leverage Engaging Intros and Outros*
Create a memorable podcast experience with engaging intros and outros. Hook your listeners from the start, and leave them with a clear call to action at the end. Intros set the tone, and outros guide listeners toward further engagement or monetization avenues.

Example: Include a brief teaser of the episode content in the intro to grab attention.

6. *Monetize Through Sponsorships and Ads*
Explore sponsorship and advertising opportunities to monetize your podcast. As your listener base grows, companies may be interested in promoting their products or services to your audience. Be strategic in selecting sponsors that align with your podcast's theme.

Pro Tip: Platforms like Anchor and Podbean offer built-in tools to connect podcasters with potential sponsors.

7. Create Bonus Content and Premium Memberships

Reward your most loyal listeners with bonus content or premium memberships. Offer exclusive episodes, behind-the-scenes insights, or early access as perks for subscribers. This strategy not only adds value for your audience but also generates additional income.

Example: If you host a storytelling podcast, offer extended interviews or additional stories for premium members.

Recap: Podcasting Profits Unlocked

To sum it up:
- Define a clear niche and target audience for your podcast.
- Develop a consistent and compelling content strategy.
- Invest in quality audio equipment for professional sound.
- Design an eye-catching and reflective podcast cover.
- Create engaging intros and outros for a memorable experience.
- Monetize through sponsorships and advertising.
- Explore bonus content and premium memberships for added value.

Now, let's chat!
- What niche will your podcast focus on, and why?
- How can you incorporate engaging intros and outros into your podcast?

In our next chapter, we'll delve into the world of advanced podcast monetization strategies. Get ready to elevate your podcasting venture to new heights of profitability! Your journey to podcasting for profit is on the brink of exciting possibilities.

Monetization Models for Podcasters

Hello Monetization Maestros! In this chapter, we're unraveling the diverse and lucrative ways podcasters can turn their passion for podcasting into a sustainable income stream. Whether you're a veteran podcaster or just launching your first episodes, let's explore the monetization models that can elevate your podcasting venture to new financial heights:

1. Sponsorships and Advertising
One of the most common and accessible monetization models for podcasters is securing sponsorships and advertising deals. Companies pay to have their products or services promoted on your podcast. As your listener base grows, you become an attractive platform for potential sponsors.

Pro Tip: Tailor sponsorships to align with your podcast's niche for more effective partnerships.

2. Listener Donations and Crowdfunding
Engage your audience directly by incorporating listener donations and crowdfunding campaigns. Platforms like Patreon allow your loyal listeners to contribute financially to support your podcast. Offer exclusive perks,

such as bonus episodes or behind-the-scenes content, to incentivize contributions.

Example: Create different donation tiers with varying perks to cater to different audience segments.

3. Premium Memberships and Subscription Models

Introduce premium memberships or subscription models for your podcast. Offer exclusive content, early access to episodes, or ad-free listening as perks for subscribers. This model provides a recurring revenue stream while providing added value to your dedicated audience.

Pro Tip: Regularly update and refresh premium content to keep subscribers engaged.

4. Affiliate Marketing on Podcasts

Similar to blogs and websites, podcasters can venture into affiliate marketing. Promote products or services related to your podcast's theme and earn a commission for every sale made through your unique affiliate link. Choose affiliates that resonate with your audience for optimal results.

Example: If you're a fitness podcaster, partner with health and wellness affiliates.

5. Selling Merchandise
Transform your podcast brand into tangible products. Design and sell merchandise such as branded t-shirts, mugs, or stickers. Merchandise not only provides an additional revenue stream but also serves as a promotional tool for your podcast.

Pro Tip: Collaborate with a print-on-demand service to minimize inventory management.

6. Live Events and Workshops
Take your podcast to the stage by organizing live events or workshops. Charge admission fees for exclusive live recordings, Q&A sessions, or educational workshops. Engaging with your audience in person adds a personal touch and generates revenue.

Example: If you host a comedy podcast, organize live stand-up shows featuring your podcast hosts.

7. Licensing and Syndication
Explore licensing your podcast content to other platforms or networks. Syndicating your episodes to multiple platforms can open up

opportunities for revenue-sharing agreements. This model requires negotiating deals that benefit both parties involved.

Pro Tip: Retain control over the rights to your content while exploring syndication options.

Recap: Turning Podcasting into Profits

To summarize:
- Secure sponsorships and advertising deals.
- Encourage listener donations and crowdfunding.
- Introduce premium memberships and subscription models.
- Venture into affiliate marketing with relevant partners.
- Sell branded merchandise to your podcast audience.
- Organize live events or workshops for additional revenue.
- Explore licensing and syndication opportunities for wider reach.

Now, let's chat!
- Which monetization model aligns best with your podcasting goals?
- How can you leverage multiple models to diversify your podcast's revenue streams?

Building a Loyal Podcast Audience

Greetings Podcasting Architects! In this chapter, we're delving into the art and science of cultivating a dedicated and engaged podcast audience. Building a loyal community not only enhances the impact of your podcast but also creates a foundation for sustained success. Let's explore the strategies to foster a strong bond with your listeners:

1. Know Your Audience Intimately
Understanding your audience is the bedrock of loyalty. Dive deep into the demographics, interests, and preferences of your listeners. Conduct surveys, engage in social media conversations, and actively seek feedback to tailor your content to their desires.

Example: If your podcast is about technology, inquire about specific tech interests through social media polls.

2. Consistency is the Key
Consistency builds trust and reliability. Stick to a regular release schedule, whether it's weekly, bi-weekly, or monthly. Reliable and predictable

content delivery keeps your audience eagerly anticipating each episode.

Pro Tip: Inform your audience of any schedule changes and provide a transparent communication channel.

3. Interact Through Social Media and Community Platforms

Extend the conversation beyond the podcast by actively engaging with your audience on social media platforms. Create a dedicated community where listeners can connect, share insights, and discuss episodes. Respond to comments, ask questions, and make your audience feel heard.

Example: Create a Facebook Group or Discord channel for your podcast community to flourish.

4. Humanize Your Podcast

Inject a human touch into your podcast. Share personal anecdotes, experiences, and even bloopers. This vulnerability creates a relatable connection with your audience, fostering a sense of friendship and loyalty.

Pro Tip: Consider occasional Q&A episodes where you answer questions from your audience.

5. Seek and Showcase Listener Contributions

Empower your audience to contribute to your podcast. Encourage them to send in questions, share stories, or even record short messages that you can feature in your episodes. This active involvement deepens their investment in your podcast.

Example: Dedicate a segment of your podcast to listener stories or questions.

6. Offer Exclusive Content and Benefits Reward your most loyal listeners with exclusive content or perks. This could be bonus episodes, early access to content, or special behind-the-scenes insights. Creating a sense of exclusivity strengthens the bond with your dedicated audience.

Pro Tip: Tie exclusive content to premium memberships for added value.

7. Adapt and Grow with Listener Feedback
Your audience's feedback is invaluable. Actively seek feedback through surveys, social media, or direct messages. Use this input to adapt and improve your podcast. Showing that you value their opinions makes listeners feel invested in the growth of your show.

Example: Ask for feedback on specific segments or topics to gauge audience preferences.

Recap: Architecting Podcast Loyalty

To recap:
- Know your audience intimately through surveys and engagement.
- Maintain consistency in your release schedule.
- Actively interact with your audience on social media and community platforms.
- Humanize your podcast by sharing personal stories and experiences.
- Showcase listener contributions to deepen their involvement.
- Offer exclusive content and benefits to reward loyalty.
- Adapt and grow with listener feedback for continuous improvement.

Now, let's chat!
- How do you currently engage with your podcast audience?
- What exclusive content or perks can you offer to enhance loyalty?

In our next chapter, we'll explore advanced audience-building strategies to elevate your podcast to new heights. Get ready to witness your podcast community flourish! Your journey to building a loyal podcast audience is on the path to lasting success.

Chapter 7

Strategies for Successful Email Marketing

Building an Email List

Greetings Email Marketing Enthusiasts! In this chapter, we're diving into the powerful realm of email marketing, a cornerstone for building lasting connections with your audience. Our focus today is on the essential step of building an email list. Let's explore the strategies to construct a robust and engaged email subscriber base:

1. Create Compelling Lead Magnets
Entice your audience to join your email list by offering valuable lead magnets. These can be e-books, guides, templates, or exclusive content that addresses the needs and interests of your target audience. A compelling lead magnet is the key to capturing those coveted email addresses.

Pro Tip: Ensure your lead magnet aligns with the themes of your content and provides genuine value.

2. Design Visually Appealing Opt-In Forms
The gateway to your email list is your opt-in form. Design visually appealing and user-friendly forms that seamlessly integrate with your website or landing pages. Communicate the benefits of subscribing and make the opt-in process straightforward.

Example: Use contrasting colors for your CTA button to make it stand out on the page.

3. Implement Exit-Intent Popups
Capture the attention of website visitors who are about to leave with exit-intent popups. These popups appear when a user is showing signs of leaving your site, providing a last-minute opportunity to encourage them to subscribe to your email list.

Pro Tip: Offer a special discount, freebie, or exclusive content in exit-intent popups to entice sign-ups.

4. Leverage Content Upgrades
Enhance the value of your blog posts or content by offering content upgrades. These are specific

bonuses or additional resources related to the content the visitor is consuming. To access these upgrades, users must subscribe to your email list.

Example: If you have a blog post on "Top 10 Productivity Tips," offer a downloadable checklist as a content upgrade.

5. Run Contests and Giveaways

Create excitement and encourage participation by running contests or giveaways. Require participants to enter using their email addresses. This not only builds your email list but also generates buzz around your brand.

Pro Tip: Ensure that the prize is relevant to your target audience to attract quality leads.

6. Utilize Social Media Integration

Extend your reach by integrating email sign-up opportunities into your social media channels. Create posts or ads that promote your lead magnets, contests, or exclusive content, directing followers to subscribe to your email list.

Example: Pin a tweet or post on Facebook promoting your latest lead magnet.

7. Offer Exclusive Early Access or Discounts

Incentivize subscribers with exclusive perks such as early access to new content, products, or special discounts. The promise of exclusive benefits encourages people to join your email list to access these privileges.

Pro Tip: communicate the ongoing value of being part of your email community.

Recap: Crafting an Engaged Email List

To summarize:
- Create compelling lead magnets that align with your audience's needs.
- Design visually appealing opt-in forms for a seamless user experience.
- Implement exit-intent popups to capture departing visitors.
- Enhance blog posts with content upgrades for added value.
- Run contests and giveaways to generate excitement and sign-ups.
- Integrate email sign-up opportunities into your social media channels.
- Offer exclusive early access or discounts to incentivize subscriptions.

Now, let's chat!
- What lead magnet could you create to entice your target audience?
- How can you integrate email sign-up opportunities into your social media strategy?

In our next chapter, we'll explore advanced email marketing strategies to transform your subscribers into engaged and loyal fans. Get ready to elevate your email marketing game! Your journey to successful email marketing is entering a phase of strategic growth and engagement.

Crafting Effective Email Campaigns

Hello, Email Campaign Architects! In this chapter, we'll dive into the art and science of crafting email campaigns that captivate your audience, drive engagement, and achieve your desired outcomes. Whether you're promoting a product, sharing valuable content, or nurturing relationships, let's explore the strategies to create email campaigns that resonate with your subscribers:

1. Define Clear Objectives
Before you start crafting your email, define clear and specific objectives. Are you aiming to drive sales, increase brand awareness, or nurture leads? Having a well-defined goal guides the content and structure of your email campaign.

Pro Tip: Align your objectives with the stage of the buyer's journey your audience is in.

2. Segment Your Audience
Personalization is the key to impactful email campaigns. Segment your email list based on demographics, behavior, or preferences. Tailor your content to each segment, delivering messages that resonate with the unique needs of different audience groups.

Example: If you have a clothing brand, segment your list based on preferences like casual wear or formal attire.

3. Craft Compelling Subject Lines
The subject line is your first impression. Craft subject lines that are attention-grabbing, concise, and relevant to the content of your email. Experiment with personalization, urgency, or curiosity to entice subscribers to open your emails.

Pro Tip: Test different subject lines to discover what resonates best with your audience.

4. Focus on Engaging Content
Deliver content that is valuable, relevant, and engaging. Whether it's a promotional offer, educational content, or a newsletter, ensure that your email provides meaningful value to your subscribers. Use a conversational tone and keep your messaging clear.

Example: If you're promoting a new product, highlight its unique features and benefits.

5. Incorporate Visual Appeal
Humans are visual creatures. Enhance the visual appeal of your emails with compelling graphics, images, and a well-designed layout. Use visuals

to complement your message and guide the reader's attention.

Pro Tip: Optimize images for fast loading times to ensure a smooth user experience.

6. Call-to-Action Excellence

Every email should have a clear and compelling call-to-action (CTA). Whether it's to shop now, read more, or subscribe, make your CTA stand out. Use buttons, contrasting colors, and persuasive language to encourage clicks.

Example: Instead of "Learn More," try "Discover Exclusive Insights."

7. Mobile Optimization

With a significant portion of email opens occurring on mobile devices, it's crucial to optimize your emails for mobile responsiveness. Ensure that your emails look and function seamlessly on various screen sizes.

Pro Tip: Test your emails on different devices to guarantee a consistent experience.

Recap: Mastering Email Campaigns

To sum it up:

- Define clear objectives for your email campaign.
- Segment your audience for personalized messaging.
- Craft attention-grabbing subject lines.
- Focus on delivering engaging and valuable content.
- Incorporate visually appealing graphics and layout.
- Include a clear and compelling call to action.
- Optimize your emails for mobile responsiveness.

Now, let's chat!
- What objectives are you aiming to achieve with your next email campaign?
- How can you enhance personalization in your segmented email content?

In our next chapter, we'll explore advanced strategies to automate and optimize your email campaigns for efficiency and effectiveness. Get ready to elevate your email marketing prowess! Your journey to crafting effective email campaigns is on the path to strategic success.

Monetizing Through Email Marketing

Hello Monetization Maestros! In this chapter, we're delving into the powerful realm of turning your email marketing efforts into revenue-generating opportunities. Your email list is not just a list; it's a valuable asset that can contribute significantly to your financial success. Let's explore the strategies to monetize through email marketing:

1. Promotional Campaigns and Product Launches

Leverage your email list to promote products or services. Craft compelling promotional campaigns or announcements for new product launches. Use persuasive language, highlight key features, and include exclusive offers to drive conversions.

Pro Tip: Create a sense of urgency with limited-time offers to encourage immediate action.

2. Affiliate Marketing Collaborations

Integrate affiliate marketing into your email strategy by promoting products or services from partners. Ensure that the affiliate offerings align with the interests and needs of your audience.

Earn commissions for every sale generated through your unique affiliate links.

Example: If you're a lifestyle blogger, collaborate with affiliates offering relevant products like fashion or wellness items.

3. Exclusive Discounts for Subscribers

Reward your email subscribers with exclusive discounts. Whether it's a seasonal sale, special promotion, or a loyalty discount, make your subscribers feel valued. Exclusive discounts create a sense of privilege and can drive repeat purchases.

Pro Tip: Use personalized discount codes for a more individualized touch.

4. Webinars and Online Courses

Monetize your expertise by offering webinars or online courses to your email subscribers. Provide valuable insights, tutorials, or in-depth training sessions. Charge a fee for access, and use your email list to promote and fill up your virtual classrooms.

Example: If you're a digital marketing expert, offer a series of webinars on advanced strategies.

5. Membership or Subscription Models

Introduce membership or subscription models to your audience. Offer premium content, early access, or exclusive perks to subscribers who opt for a monthly or yearly subscription. This model provides a recurring revenue stream.

Pro Tip: Clearly communicate the ongoing value of the membership to retain subscribers.

6. Sponsored Emails and Collaborations

Monetize your email list by collaborating with sponsors. Feature sponsored content or announcements in your email newsletters. Ensure that sponsored content aligns with your brand and offers value to your subscribers.

Example: If you're a travel blogger, collaborate with travel brands for sponsored destination features.

7. Upselling and Cross-Selling

Maximize revenue from your existing customers by implementing upselling and cross-selling strategies. Recommend complementary products or premium upgrades to your subscribers based on their previous purchases or interactions.

Pro Tip: Use data analytics to identify upselling and cross-selling opportunities effectively.

Recap: Transforming Emails into Revenue Streams

To summarize:
- Utilize promotional campaigns and product launches.
- Integrate affiliate marketing collaborations with relevant partners.
- Offer exclusive discounts as a reward for subscriber loyalty.
- Monetize expertise through webinars and online courses.
- Introduce membership or subscription models for recurring revenue.
- Collaborate with sponsors for sponsored emails and content.
- Implement upselling and cross-selling strategies for increased sales.

Now, let's chat!
- Which monetization strategy aligns best with your business or content?
- How can you strategically implement these strategies into your email marketing campaigns?

In our final chapter, we'll explore advanced tactics to optimize and scale your email marketing monetization efforts. Get ready to witness the full potential of your email list as a revenue-generating powerhouse! Your journey to monetizing through email marketing is reaching its pinnacle of strategic success.

Chapter 8

Diversifying Income Streams

The Power of Multiple Income Streams

Greetings Income Diversifiers! In this pivotal chapter, we'll explore the transformative impact of cultivating multiple income streams. Diversification is not just a financial strategy; it's a powerful approach to safeguarding and amplifying your overall success. Let's delve into the importance, benefits, and strategies of embracing the dynamic world of multiple income streams:

1. The Significance of Diversification
Diversifying income streams is akin to planting seeds in various fields. It guards against the volatility of relying solely on one source of revenue. By creating a diversified portfolio of income streams, you not only mitigate risks but also open doors to new opportunities and financial growth.

Pro Tip: Think of each income stream as a building block, contributing to the robust structure of your overall financial stability.

2. Benefits of Multiple Income Streams
Risk Mitigation: When one income stream faces challenges, others can provide a buffer, ensuring a more stable financial standing.

Adaptability: Different income streams respond differently to market changes. Diversification allows you to adapt to evolving trends and economic shifts.

Increased Financial Growth: With multiple streams, your overall income potential expands. This provides room for scaling and achieving higher financial goals.

3. Types of Income Streams to Explore
Active Income: Directly trading time for money through services or employment.

Passive Income: Earnings generated with minimal ongoing effort, such as investments or royalties.

Residual Income: Continual income from past efforts, common in industries like writing or digital products.

Portfolio Income: Returns from investments like stocks, bonds, or real estate.

4. Strategies for Creating Multiple Income Streams

Identify Your Strengths: Determine your skills, expertise, and passions. What can you offer in various areas?

Explore Niche Opportunities: Investigate niche markets or underserved areas where your skills can fill a gap.

Leverage Digital Platforms: Capitalize on online platforms for freelancing, selling products, or offering digital services.

Invest Smartly: Explore investment opportunities, diversifying between stocks, real estate, and other vehicles.

Build Passive Income Sources: Consider creating digital products, writing books, or investing in ventures that generate passive income.

5. Balancing Time and Effort

Diversifying income streams requires strategic time management. Allocate your time effectively among different ventures, ensuring each receives the attention necessary for growth. Strike a balance between active and passive income pursuits.

Pro Tip: Use productivity tools and scheduling techniques to optimize your time.

6. Continuous Learning and Adaptation

The landscape of income generation evolves. Stay informed, be open to learning, and adapt your strategies accordingly. Embrace a mindset of continuous improvement and explore emerging opportunities in your chosen fields.

Example: If you're a content creator, stay updated on new platforms, content formats, and monetization methods.

Recap: Unleashing the Power of Diversity

In summary:
- Understand the significance of diversifying income streams for financial stability.
- Reap the benefits of risk mitigation, adaptability, and increased financial growth.
- Explore various types of income streams, including active, passive, residual, and portfolio income.
- Strategize by identifying strengths, exploring niches, leveraging digital platforms, and making smart investments.
- Balance time and effort effectively among diverse income pursuits.

- Embrace continuous learning and adaptation to stay ahead in the ever-evolving landscape.

Now, let's chat!
- Which types of income streams resonate most with your skills and interests?
- How can you strategically implement diversification into your current income strategy?

In our final chapter, we'll explore advanced tactics for optimizing and scaling your diversified income streams. Get ready to unlock the full potential of your multifaceted financial portfolio! Your journey to mastering the power of multiple income streams is on the cusp of exponential growth.

Investing in Passive Income Opportunities

Greetings Passive Income Enthusiasts! In this chapter, we'll embark on a journey into the realm of investing in opportunities that generate passive income, a pathway to financial freedom and long-term wealth. Let's explore the strategies, considerations, and potential avenues for smartly investing in passive income opportunities:

1. Understanding Passive Income Investments

Passive income investments involve putting your money to work to generate returns with minimal ongoing effort. Unlike active income, where you trade time for money, passive income allows you to build wealth while maintaining flexibility.

Pro Tip: A diversified portfolio often includes a mix of passive income streams for stability.

2. Types of Passive Income Investments

Dividend Stocks: Invest in stocks of companies that distribute a portion of their earnings as dividends. Regular dividend payments provide a steady income stream.

Real Estate Investments: Owning rental properties or investing in Real Estate Investment Trusts (REITs) can yield rental income and potential appreciation.

Peer-to-Peer Lending: Lend money to individuals or small businesses through online platforms, earning interest on your loans.

Create and Sell Digital Products: Develop digital products like e-books, online courses, or software, and earn royalties with each sale.

Stock Market Investments: Beyond dividends, capital gains from buying and selling stocks can contribute to passive income.

3. Risk Mitigation and Due Diligence

All investments come with risks, and it's crucial to conduct thorough due diligence. Understand the risks associated with each investment type, diversify your portfolio, and stay informed about market trends.

Example: Before investing in a REIT, research the real estate market, the specific properties in the portfolio, and the track record of the management team.

4. Creating a Diversified Portfolio

Diversification is a key strategy for managing risk. Spread your investments across different asset classes and industries to ensure that the performance of one does not overly impact your entire portfolio.

Pro Tip: Regularly review and rebalance your portfolio based on changing market conditions.

5. Passive Income from Digital Assets

In the digital age, creating and selling digital assets can be a lucrative form of passive income. Develop an online course, write an e-book, or design and sell digital art. The initial effort is substantial, but once created, these assets can generate income over time.

Example: If you have expertise in a specific field, consider creating an online course and selling it on platforms like Udemy or Teachable.

6. Reinvesting Passive Income

Maximize the power of compounding by reinvesting the passive income you earn. Reinvesting can accelerate the growth of your portfolio over time, especially when returns are compounded.

Pro Tip: Consider using dividend reinvestment plans (DRIPs) offered by some companies to automatically reinvest dividends.

Recap: Navigating the Passive Income Investment Landscape

In summary:
- Understand the concept and benefits of passive income investments.
- Explore various types, including dividend stocks, real estate, peer-to-peer lending, and digital products.
- Mitigate risks through thorough due diligence and a diversified portfolio.
- Leverage the power of compounding by reinvesting passive income.
- Stay informed about market trends and regularly review and rebalance your portfolio.

Now, let's chat!
- Which passive income opportunities align with your financial goals and risk tolerance?
- How can you strategically diversify your portfolio to optimize returns?

Future Trends in Online Monetization

Hello, Futurists of Online Monetization! In this concluding chapter, we'll embark on a journey into the anticipated trends that will shape the landscape of online monetization in the coming years. Stay ahead of the curve by exploring these emerging trends and positioning yourself for success in the evolving digital economy:

1. Decentralized Finance (DeFi) and Cryptocurrency

The rise of decentralized finance (DeFi) and the increasing acceptance of cryptocurrency are reshaping financial transactions. Smart contracts, blockchain, and decentralized applications (DApps) are offering new avenues for creators to monetize their content and services without relying on traditional financial institutions.

Pro Tip: Stay informed about the regulatory landscape and security measures in the crypto space.

2. Subscription-Based Models with Niche Focus

As online content continues to diversify, subscription-based models are becoming more prevalent. Creators are finding success by offering niche-focused subscription services, providing exclusive content, community access, or specialized expertise to a dedicated audience.

Example: Niche subscription boxes, premium content memberships, and specialized knowledge platforms.

3. Virtual and Augmented Reality (VR/AR) Experiences

The immersive nature of VR and AR technologies is unlocking new monetization possibilities. Creators and businesses can offer virtual experiences, events, and products, creating unique opportunities for monetization through virtual marketplaces, events, and enhanced digital interactions.

Pro Tip: Explore partnerships with VR/AR developers to integrate immersive experiences into your offerings.

4. Interactive and Live Content Monetization

Audiences are craving more interactive and live content experiences. Creators can monetize live streams, Q&A sessions, and interactive events through various means, including virtual gifts, tips, and exclusive access tiers.

Example: Platforms like Twitch and YouTube Live are popular for interactive content monetization.

5. *Artificial Intelligence (AI) and Personalization*

AI-driven personalization is enhancing user experiences and creating new avenues for targeted advertising and product recommendations. Creators can leverage AI algorithms to tailor content and offers, increasing engagement and conversion rates.

Pro Tip: Invest in AI tools that enhance user experience and automate personalized content delivery.

6. *Non-Fungible Tokens (NFTs) and Digital Collectibles*

NFTs have disrupted the digital art and collectibles market, enabling creators to tokenize and sell unique digital assets. From digital art to virtual real estate, NFTs provide a decentralized and transparent way to monetize digital creations.

Example: Creators can tokenize exclusive content or digital assets as limited edition NFTs.

7. *Ephemeral Content and FOMO Marketing*

Ephemeral content, which disappears after a short period, creates a sense of urgency and exclusivity. Creators can leverage FOMO (Fear of Missing Out) marketing strategies to monetize time-sensitive offers, limited-time discounts, and exclusive access.

Pro Tip: Use social media stories and short-lived content to drive FOMO and increase engagement.

Recap: Navigating the Future of Online Monetization

To summarize:

- Embrace decentralized finance (DeFi) and explore cryptocurrency opportunities.
- Consider niche-focused subscription models for exclusive content and community access.
- Explore monetization possibilities in virtual and augmented reality experiences.
- Leverage interactive and live content for audience engagement and monetization.
- Harness the power of AI for personalized content and advertising.
- Explore NFTs and digital collectibles for unique monetization avenues.

- Embrace ephemeral content and FOMO marketing for time-sensitive offers.

Now, let's chat!
- Which future trend resonates most with your content or business model?
- How can you prepare and position yourself for success in the evolving landscape of online monetization?

Congratulations on completing this comprehensive guide to online monetization! May your journey be filled with innovation, success, and the realization of your financial aspirations in the dynamic world of digital entrepreneurship.

Chapter 9

Overcoming Challenges and Pitfalls

Common Mistakes to Avoid

Hello Resilient Entrepreneurs! In this critical chapter, we'll navigate the common challenges and pitfalls that can hinder your journey to online monetization success. Learn from the experiences of others and equip yourself with strategies to overcome obstacles. Let's delve into the potential pitfalls and the proactive measures to ensure a smoother path to your digital aspirations:

1. Lack of Clear Monetization Strategy
Pitfall: Many entrepreneurs falter by diving into the digital landscape without a well-defined monetization strategy. Without clarity on how to generate revenue, efforts may scatter, and results may fall short of expectations.

Solution: Begin with a clear and comprehensive monetization strategy. Identify your target audience, choose suitable revenue streams, and outline a step-by-step plan to achieve your financial goals.

2. Ignoring Audience Engagement

Pitfall: Neglecting audience engagement can lead to reduced traffic, diminishing trust, and missed monetization opportunities. Building a passive audience is a recipe for stagnation.

Solution: Prioritize engagement through interactive content, social media interactions, and community building. An engaged audience is more likely to convert into loyal customers and consistent revenue.

3. Inadequate Investment in Marketing

Pitfall: Even the most valuable products or services can go unnoticed without effective marketing. Underestimating the importance of marketing can result in low visibility and limited monetization.

Solution: Allocate sufficient resources to marketing efforts. Utilize social media, content marketing, SEO, and other digital marketing strategies to enhance visibility and reach your target audience.

4. Overlooking SEO and Website Optimization

Pitfall: A beautifully designed website is only effective if it's easily discoverable. Ignoring search engine optimization (SEO) and website optimization can lead to poor search rankings and decreased traffic.

Solution: Invest in SEO practices, optimize your website for speed and mobile users, and ensure a user-friendly experience. A well-optimized site is more likely to attract organic traffic and support your monetization efforts.

5. Neglecting Analytics and Data

Pitfall: Overlooking the power of analytics and data can leave you in the dark about what is working and what needs improvement. Without insights, you may miss opportunities for optimization.

Solution: Implement robust analytics tools to track user behavior, engagement, and conversion metrics. Regularly analyze data to make informed decisions and continuously refine your strategies.

6. Impatience and Unrealistic Expectations

Pitfall: Online monetization is a journey, not a sprint. Impatience and setting unrealistic expectations can lead to disappointment and premature abandonment of potentially successful ventures.

Solution: Set realistic short-term and long-term goals. Understand that success takes time, and consistent effort is key. Celebrate small victories along the way and stay committed to your journey.

7. Failing to Adapt to Changes
Pitfall: The digital landscape evolves rapidly. Failing to adapt to changes, whether in technology, consumer behavior, or market trends, can leave your strategies outdated.

Solution: Stay informed about industry trends, technology advancements, and shifts in consumer behavior. Be adaptable and open to refining your strategies to align with changing circumstances.

Recap: Navigating Challenges and Avoiding Pitfalls

To sum it up:
- Develop a clear monetization strategy to guide your efforts.
- Prioritize audience engagement for a loyal and active community.

- Allocate sufficient resources to marketing for increased visibility.
- Focus on SEO and website optimization to enhance discoverability.
- Embrace analytics and data to make informed decisions.
- Set realistic expectations and remain patient on your journey.
- Stay adaptable and be open to refining strategies based on changing circumstances.

Now, let's chat!
- Have you encountered any of these pitfalls in your online monetization journey?
- How can you proactively address these challenges and steer your path towards success?

Adapting to Changes in the Online Landscape

Greetings Agile Entrepreneurs! In this pivotal chapter, we'll delve into the art of adaptation, a fundamental skill for navigating the ever-evolving online landscape. Embracing change is not just a necessity but a strategic advantage in the dynamic digital realm. Let's explore why adaptation is crucial, how to identify changes, and strategies to stay ahead:

1. The Imperative of Adaptation
Why Adaptation Matters: The online landscape is a constantly shifting terrain influenced by technology, consumer behavior, and market trends. Those who embrace change proactively position themselves for success, while those resistant to change risk becoming obsolete.

Strategy: Cultivate a mindset that views change as an opportunity rather than a threat. Understand that adaptation is not just about survival but about thriving in the face of new possibilities.

2. Identifying Key Changes
Technology Shifts: Keep an eye on emerging technologies that can impact your industry.

From AI and blockchain to new software tools, staying informed is crucial.

Consumer Behavior: Understand how your target audience consumes content and makes purchasing decisions. Rapid shifts in consumer behavior can open new avenues for monetization.

Market Trends: Regularly analyze market trends and industry reports. Identifying early signs of emerging trends allows you to position your strategies accordingly.

3. Staying Informed and Connected
Industry Forums and Networks: Engage with industry forums, conferences, and networks to stay updated on the latest developments. Connect with peers and thought leaders to gain insights and share knowledge.

Continuous Learning: Embrace a culture of continuous learning. Enroll in courses, webinars, or workshops to deepen your understanding of new technologies and trends.

4. Flexibility in Strategy and Execution
Agile Planning: Adopt agile planning methodologies. Break down long-term plans into

smaller, flexible milestones that can adapt to changing circumstances.

Pilot Programs: Test new strategies or technologies through pilot programs. This allows you to assess viability before full-scale implementation.

5. Customer Feedback and Iteration
Feedback Loops: Establish robust feedback loops with your audience. Regularly seek customer feedback to understand their evolving needs and expectations.

Iterative Processes: Implement iterative processes in product development and marketing. Continuously refine your offerings based on real-time feedback.

6. Building a Culture of Innovation
Encouraging Innovation: Foster a culture that encourages innovation. Empower your team to propose and experiment with new ideas without fear of failure.

Rewarding Innovation: Recognize and reward innovative efforts. This motivates your team to proactively contribute to the company's adaptive culture.

Recap: *Mastering Adaptation in the Digital Realm*

To summarize:
- Understand why adaptation is crucial for sustained success.
- Identify key changes in technology, consumer behavior, and market trends.
- Stay informed through industry forums, continuous learning, and networking.
- Plan flexibly, with the ability to adjust strategies based on changing circumstances.
- Establish feedback loops with customers and implement iterative processes.
- Build a culture that encourages innovation and rewards creative efforts.

Now, let's chat!
- How do you currently stay informed about changes in your industry?
- What steps can you take to foster a culture of innovation within your team?

Navigating Legal and Ethical Considerations

Greetings Agile Entrepreneurs! In this pivotal chapter, we'll delve into the art of adaptation, a fundamental skill for navigating the ever-evolving online landscape. Embracing change is not just a necessity but a strategic advantage in the dynamic digital realm. Let's explore why adaptation is crucial, how to identify changes, and strategies to stay ahead:

1. The Imperative of Adaptation

Why Adaptation Matters: The online landscape is a constantly shifting terrain influenced by technology, consumer behavior, and market trends. Those who embrace change proactively position themselves for success, while those resistant to change risk becoming obsolete.

Strategy: Cultivate a mindset that views change as an opportunity rather than a threat. Understand that adaptation is not just about survival but about thriving in the face of new possibilities.

2. Identifying Key Changes

Technology Shifts: Keep an eye on emerging technologies that can impact your industry.

From AI and blockchain to new software tools, staying informed is crucial.

Consumer Behavior: Understand how your target audience consumes content and makes purchasing decisions. Rapid shifts in consumer behavior can open new avenues for monetization.

Market Trends: Regularly analyze market trends and industry reports. Identifying early signs of emerging trends allows you to position your strategies accordingly.

3. Staying Informed and Connected
Industry Forums and Networks: Engage with industry forums, conferences, and networks to stay updated on the latest developments. Connect with peers and thought leaders to gain insights and share knowledge.

Continuous Learning: Embrace a culture of continuous learning. Enroll in courses, webinars, or workshops to deepen your understanding of new technologies and trends.

4. Flexibility in Strategy and Execution
Agile Planning: Adopt agile planning methodologies. Break down long-term plans into

smaller, flexible milestones that can adapt to changing circumstances.

Pilot Programs: Test new strategies or technologies through pilot programs. This allows you to assess viability before full-scale implementation.

5. Customer Feedback and Iteration
Feedback Loops: Establish robust feedback loops with your audience. Regularly seek customer feedback to understand their evolving needs and expectations.

Iterative Processes: Implement iterative processes in product development and marketing. Continuously refine your offerings based on real-time feedback.

6. Building a Culture of Innovation
Encouraging Innovation: Foster a culture that encourages innovation. Empower your team to propose and experiment with new ideas without fear of failure.

Rewarding Innovation: Recognize and reward innovative efforts. This motivates your team to proactively contribute to the company's adaptive culture.

Recap: *Mastering Adaptation in the Digital Realm*

To summarize:
- Understand why adaptation is crucial for sustained success.
- Identify key changes in technology, consumer behavior, and market trends.
- Stay informed through industry forums, continuous learning, and networking.
- Plan flexibly, with the ability to adjust strategies based on changing circumstances.
- Establish feedback loops with customers and implement iterative processes.
- Build a culture that encourages innovation and rewards creative efforts.

Now, let's chat!
- How do you currently stay informed about changes in your industry?
- What steps can you take to foster a culture of innovation within your team?

In our final chapter, we'll explore advanced strategies for mastering adaptation and future-proofing your online monetization endeavors. Get ready to lead the charge in the dynamic digital landscape! Your journey to mastering adaptation in the online world is a continuous evolution toward strategic excellence.

Conclusion

As we conclude our comprehensive guide, "Online Riches in 2024: The Comprehensive Guide to Monetizing Websites, Blogging, Video, and More for Income," we reflect on the transformative journey we've embarked upon together. In the dynamic digital landscape, where change is the only constant, you, dear reader, have armed yourself with the knowledge, strategies, and insights needed to thrive.

Our exploration began by painting a compelling vision of financial freedom through online ventures, unveiling the current opportunities that abound in the rapidly evolving internet sphere. We established credibility by delving into my own experiences and credentials, creating a foundation of trust for the insightful guidance that followed.

Throughout our chapters, we navigated the essentials of building a strong online presence, crafting compelling content, and leveraging various monetization strategies, from ads and affiliate marketing to blogging, video creation, and podcasting. We explored the power of email marketing, diversified income streams, and the intricacies of investing for passive income.

In the pursuit of success, we confronted challenges head-on, learning from common mistakes, and discovering the art of adaptation, a skill essential for staying ahead in the ever-shifting online landscape. We peeked into the future, exploring trends that will shape the digital terrain in the years to come.

Now, armed with a robust toolkit of knowledge, strategies, and a mindset poised for adaptation, you stand at the threshold of your digital destiny. Your journey towards online riches is not just a quest for financial gain but a dynamic exploration of the limitless possibilities the digital world presents.

As you turn the final page of this guide, remember that success in the online realm is not just about the destination but the continuous evolution of your strategies, the resilience to overcome challenges, and the foresight to embrace change. The future is yours to shape, and the digital horizon awaits your innovative endeavors.

May your online ventures be prosperous, your creativity boundless, and your journey toward online riches be a testament to the limitless potential that resides within you. Thank you for joining us on this enriching expedition, and may your digital odyssey be filled with abundance and success.

Here's to your online riches in 2024 and beyond!

Warm regards,